11+ A Kid's Experience for Children and Their Parents

An easy to follow explanation and a
true story of the 11+ process

Tom and Imelda Chavez-O'Reilly
June 2012

Contents

Prologue

Hi, my name is Tom and I have just finished doing my 11+ exams and I would like to tell you all what I have been doing to get this far.

First, let me tell you some things about me:

I am 11 years old; I have a little brother who is 5 and live with my Mum and Dad.

I like school most of the times. I love exercising and try to practice my favourite sports during the week.

At school, I have always been in the top tables and have enjoyed Maths very much.

I practice violin on Tuesdays during school time. I attend Judo on Tuesday evenings and had a strings orchestra group for an hour. I have football training and sometimes school football match on Wednesdays evenings. I stay for the afterschool sports club on Thursdays and attended Jujitsu classes on Friday nights. On Saturdays I used to go to tennis classes and on Sundays I have football matches.

I also enjoy playing games on my PSP, Wii and sometimes on my old Play Station 2.

I like going to the park to ride my bike, play football and go out to have fun.

I usually find myself playing some made up games with my little brother or playing football with a soft ball in the kitchen during winter.

I also have to make time to do my homework, practice violin, read and relax.

I live in the Hillingdon Borough and am not in a good catchment area. The best schools in my Borough are so popular that every year they reduce their catchment areas and my probabilities to get in any of them get thinner.

The two other ways to get a good secondary school education could be: private school or grammar school.

My parents, as many other parents, would not afford to pay for me to go to private school for the next 7 years or so.

So my best option was a grammar school.

How it started

I remember spring 2009, I was finishing year 4 and my Mum began to wonder what to do to get me the best options for secondary school. My Mum did not study secondary school in this country so she needed all the information she could get. My Dad did all his studies in the UK but the new application process was very unfamiliar to him. So it was left up to my Mum to gather information, comments and advice from friends, internet, books and schools.

The best advice one of my Mum's friends gave us was to start attending the "open evenings"(visits to secondary schools) since I was in Year 5 and not to wait until Year 6, as other parents do, trying to visit all the schools in one go at the last minute. Her friend said: "you go and visit the schools without any pressure and are more relaxed to take your time to pay attention to details, make questions and better choices". Also, you do not have to panic in case the schools you want to visit have their open evenings on the same day as you have another year to visit them.

So, the September when I started Year 5, we visited some of my preferred non-selective secondary schools. In this way, I was not worried on what to put on my application form as a preference. I was just enjoying all the visits without any rush and did not mind if there were two or more "open evenings" at the same time, I just went to my favourite ones and took note of the others I wanted to visit next time.

I made sure to take notes of the head teachers' speeches and of what I liked and disliked and put it together with each prospectus.

We did not go the grammar schools that year, we left them for the next time as some of them had open mornings during school hours and I did not want to miss school.

My Mum used to pass the advice of going to visit the secondary schools early to my friends' parents. Some of them took it and attended the open evenings and were very pleased to do it and others thought it was too early to start thinking on secondary schools. At the end of the day, they were the ones who regretted it and found themselves with less options and no time to prepare.

We knew a family who just managed to visit one school of their preferred ones and when having to complete their application form they ended putting schools that they heard people saying were good without having a clue where the schools were or if they were going to like them. When the places were allocated the child was offered one of the 5 schools they had not visited. This can be stressing, daunting and contribute to difficulties to settle into a new school.

From the visits to secondary schools we realised the school age population in my Borough was growing and the catchment areas from the best schools were being reduced. My chances to get in one of them were smaller and smaller. I am a millennium child and that makes it more difficult: there were many children born due to the millennium boom.

Some of my friends had moved house just to be in the catchment area of their preferred secondary school. My parents could not afford it so we stayed in the same house. We like it where we live.

So we thought I could have a better chance in a grammar school where the catchment areas are not the top admission criteria. We have grammar schools close to us: Slough, Buckinghamshire and Berkshire.

Tuition

My Mum asked a family whose child from my school had passed the 11+, information on how to prepare for the exams. The family recommended a tuition company in Slough. My Mum phoned them and booked me for an "assessment" in Year 4 spring term in order to know if I had a chance to pass the 11+ after a tuition course. The assessment had maths, literacy, non verbal, verbal and spelling questions.
When I finished they marked my test and one of the teachers sat with my Mum and me. The teacher explained I had a good chance but I needed to do 12 months of tuition in order to pass the tests as the verbal and non-verbal subjects are not taught in state primary schools. Unless your school is in the county where there are grammar schools.

The tuition would take place in their building on a Friday or Saturday from 10 a.m. to 3 p.m. and then I would have to do homework every day for around 60 minutes for the next 12 months! That would have meant me having to give up all my after school activities and my favourite sport: football. A part from my parents having to spend over £1,200.

Children also need to have a life, don't you agree?

A couple of my friends enrolled the 11+ tuition and had to give up their after school clubs for the whole year.

I like school and I love my Maths but I would not be happy to do all that extra tuition on the weekends and homework for a year on top of all the school work.

Dad agreed with me and was not keen on me to dedicate twelve months or more of my life doing that extra work. He insisted I was still a child. He believed children who have not got the level to go to a grammar school and are couched through excessive work to pass the 11+ and get a place in a grammar school find themselves under too much pressure to keep up with the rest of the class. Dad said it was not fair to force him/her to be in a school where the child has to suffer to catch up with the rest of the class and not enjoy the school times.

Dad mentioned the case of a friend of us who did not have the level to be in a grammar school and because of so much tuition and a sibling in a grammar school; she got a place in her preferred grammar school and had terrible time keeping up with the rest of the class. She had to have extra tuition on the weekends and was very unhappy; her self-esteem was very low and had lack of confidence.

We had heard of some cases when children attended tuition for a year or longer and got very stressed and felt the pressure and when sitting the exam they just froze and did not do well although their results during tuition were very good.

Mum went to different grammar schools websites for my area and found out they were not testing for Maths anymore and that they were testing for "verbal reasoning" and "non-verbal reasoning". As these subjects are not taught in my borough I needed to prepare for those in another way.

Ask your Mum to fully research on your preferred grammar schools as some of them still require you to sit English and Maths exams. Some schools will test you first on "verbal and non-verbal" and if you pass them then a final selection will include a Maths test.

At the start of autumn that year, my Mum went to WHSmiths to look for 11+ exams and spotted "Bond, The Parents' Stress-free Guide to the 11+" by Nelson Thornes. Mum liked the way it was structured and the explanations it had so she added it to her shopping list. After reading it, she got a clear idea of what the 11+ exam was going to be, the differences between the "verbal reasoning" and the "non-verbal reasoning" and decided to follow the structured plan suggested. [For definitions please consult the glossary at the back of this book].

My Mum also bought the "Bond How to do 11+Verbal Reasoning" and "How to do 11+ Non-verbal reasoning" both by Nelson Thornes. These books were very useful because I could find very good explanations to the different question types and were my main reference tools. Mum was very pleased with all the information, tips and recommendations these books offered.

I did the Bond Placement Tests from "The Parent's Stress-free Guide to the 11+" and when my Mum marked it she then followed the step by step guide to know what level I should start working with.

Mum consulted with my Year 4 and Year 5 teachers, analysed my schools reports and SATs results, checked my reading level and reviewed my tuition company assessment results. They all were very encouraging.

At this stage my Mum, Dad and I decided to prepare at home for the 11+ exams at my own pace and around my activities.

So my Mum bought the verbal and non-verbal "Bond Assessment Papers" for the level the Placement Test indicated and I started completing a couple of papers a week.

My Mum used to mark my papers and then together, we were analysing the questions and answers I got wrong checking with my reference tools. We could spend a few minutes checking each one of the possible answers to the questions and commenting about why they were or were not the right answers, comparing them to the answers in the "How to do..." books.

Many times we got Dad to have a go with the questions and then we were telling him the right answers.

Some of the questions were easy to answer but others were very tricky and I had to really concentrate to understand how to answer them.

In this way I managed to continue with all my activities. I just had to give up my orchestra practice on Tuesdays, but I still had the weekends for myself and football!

Even though the papers were to be answered in certain time I first concentrated on understanding how to answer them well.

My Mum got to check my work immediately after I finished the papers or when I had completed a set of them.

At the back of each book there is progress chart. I always tried to complete it when I finished each paper to keep track of my progress.

Every time I finished a book my Mum got me a treat: something that we had agreed I would get for my hard work. I got books of my favourite stories, Wii games, days out, cakes, meals out and others.

During Christmas I slowed down and enjoyed the holidays! It was time to visit friends and family, go out, play with my brother and relax with my family.

I resumed my 11+ work in January.

January

On the New Year, I had to start preparing for my violin exam and this meant less time for the 11+ but I was happy with my own personal studying plan.

By now, I knew how to tackle the "verbal" and "non-verbal" without too much consulting on my reference books. My Mum was always there to lend a helping hand to explain the tricky bits.

One of my best friends had started tuition with a private teacher near my house. His Mum told us that the tutor had asked them to buy lots of books and vocabulary books. Mum looked at the vocabulary books and found they were too many words to learn in a few months. So my Mum put together my own and personal glossary: we went through all the books and test papers and got all the words I did not know and put them together in a special list. This list used to grow by the day as I was completing more papers. My Mum typed all my words an added the meaning and example on each.

When I was answering my "verbal-reasoning" I had my list of words beside me to assist me.

At this stage I started timing myself to get an idea of how long it was taking me to complete the papers.

A few times I felt I was not learning much as I kept getting incorrect answers but my Mum was there to tell me and remind me I was getting better and learning bit by bit. Dad also tried to make me see I was improving.

Remember it is normal not to understand how to answer all the questions, just be patient because it will get easier as the days pass by and you keep practicing.

Easter

Easter arrived and after a good break attending a football camp, badminton classes and days out to my favourite theme parks I went back to my preparation. This time I was completing 3 papers a week. I always found "non-verbal" easier than "verbal" as there were always new words and codes to learn in "verbal".

I continued with school, after school activities I was finding some time to do my 11+ papers.

My Mum created a time table where she scheduled all the Bond papers I had to finish by the end of the summer in order to be ready to do the 11+ test papers.

Mum was very organised and was updating the time table every time I completed my papers. She used to explain how frequently I had to work on it.

My Mum kept in touch with her friends whose children wanted to do the 11+ exams and agreed on exchanging information of grammar schools and open evenings and looked on the websites very frequently. In that way we got to know that Slough Grammar School was having their open evening time ahead the rest of the other grammar schools. Their open evening was taking place in April while the other grammar schools were having theirs in September.

Remember that from 2012 the exam dates are different and an in few schools you have to sit the exams early September therefore the open evenings take place some months before September.

Slough Grammar Open Evening

We attended Slough open evening in April and because I had already visited Hillingdon Borough schools a year before I had a good idea of what to expect, pay attention to and compare. Once again, I took notes and sat to listen to the head teacher's speech, collected prospectus and marked Slough Grammar as one of my preferred schools. You can really notice the difference in atmosphere, pupils, behaviour, teaching level, facilities and diversity of activities from the minute you step in the grammar schools. Pupils go to school to study and go without fear of being bullied. They do not go to waste anybody's time. I could picture myself enjoying coming to this school.

During the open evening, we were informed that the 11+ exams will include a Verbal Reasoning and a Non-Verbal Reasoning Multiple-Choice tests and were advised to buy the "GL Assessment 11+ Practice Papers" Verbal Reasoning Multiple-Choice and Non-Verbal Reasoning Multiple-Choice packs to study and get an idea of how the 11+ tests for Slough Grammar would look like, they were also selling these packs in one of the classrooms. My Mum had already bought me some of those books in WHSmith therefore she just bought the ones I did not have.

It was very useful to attend the open evening as they explained what the 11+ exams were going to be and that the pass mark was 111 points. They include a "standardisation" process that relates to the age of each child. [You can find a more detailed explanation at the end of this book]. There were going to be 2 exams: Verbal and Non-Verbal Multiple-Choice and each exam would consist of 80 questions.

When we got home we checked the "GL Assessment 11+ Practice Papers" and decided not to start yet with them as I was still working with my "Bond Assessment Papers". At this time I was answering all the questions and timing myself to get used to. Sometimes I needed extra time and sometimes I did not have all the answers. My Mum always sat with me to check and understand the incorrect or unanswered questions.

At this stage I was not sure how my level in 11+ was doing as many times I was getting very good scores and others I was quite disappointed with my bad scores. I could feel I was not learning as much as I needed to do well in the exam and worried a bit but my Mum was always there to try to cheer me up and encourage me to keep trying.

It is hard to believe that you are improving when you get wrong answers but try to not be put off by it and just keep practicing, you will soon have most or all of the answers right!

May and June

I was working harder with my "Bond Assessment Papers", finishing books and starting new ones and adding new words to my vocabulary list.
I was also practicing more for my violin exam in July and having more training time for my Judo grading. Around this time I joined Jujitsu lessons on Fridays.

I also took time to attend some Judo competitions on the weekends and continued with my other activities.

During the half term we had days out to the parks and visited friends apart from spending family time at home. My Mum would not miss the opportunity to remind me of my 11+ preparation.

My Mum used to talk to other mothers about how their children were doing with their tutors to have an idea of how I should be progressing but most of them were having the same experience: very good in some papers and not too good in others. It was comforting to know that other children were in the same situation and experiencing similar feelings.

July

Now it was July and I was so much looking forward to my birthday party and my holidays in Mexico to visit my Grandparents and my Auntie. School was almost finishing. My friends and I were sad that our lovely Year 5 teacher was not going to stay teaching in our school and that we were going to have a new teacher to the school for Year 6.

Then it was time for me to have my Level 1 Violin. That day I went did my exam and went back home to do my homework and my 11+ papers.

I was relived I did not have to study anymore for my violin exam. I just had to wait for the results.

My Mum decided to post my 11+ application form for Slough Grammar before going on holidays so we could enjoy the break without worries of missing the dead line.

The weekend before school finished was very special as I had my birthday party. I did enjoy my day with some friends, their families and my family.

On the last week of classes my violin teacher went to school to inform us that I had passed my Level 1 Violin exam with merits! I was so happy. It had been worthy all the practice.

On the last school day I flew to Mexico City with my brother and my Mum. It was time to have fun and recharge the batteries.

August

We had a lovely time in Mexico City with my Grandparents and Auntie. We had time to visit different places and went to the beach in two occasions. My Mum brought with us my Bond Assessment Papers and the GL 11+ Assessment Practice Papers thinking I was going to have plenty of time to study. I did a few Bond Papers and just 1 GL Assessment Practice Paper to try to have an idea how good I was doing. My GL Assessment 11+ Practice Paper result was not as good as I thought it would be so I did not want to answer anymore of the GL Assessment Practice Papers and continued with my Bond Assessment Papers.
My little brother used to see me doing my "Verbal and Non-Verbal" paper so frequently that he decided he wanted to join me and started asking my Mum to get him his Verbal and Non-Verbal homework to do sitting beside me. He looked very serious doing his 11+ verbal and non-verbal: letter and number formation.

While in Mexico, my Mum kept in touch with my friends' Mums and one of them told her that her son's tutor had told her about the "Buckinghamshire 11+ examination". This was a surprise as we realised that if she had not informed my Mum we would not imagine I could apply for the Buckinghamshire grammar schools group. My Mum phoned my Dad in the UK and asked him to register me for the exam. My Dad registered me on the website and did not have to pay anything.

So as a note for yourself: enquiry about application forms and deadlines for the nearby counties and schools as they all differ considerably.

I consider the process for application for the 11+ tests quite tricky as there is not a central point of information and the deadlines for applications or registrations vary from school to school and from authority to authority. In this case registrations for the 11+ in Buckinghamshire were different for children attending school in that county and children like me outside the county.

Thanks to my friend's Mum, my Dad managed to register me on time, the deadline was early September. My friend's tutor recommended him to sit that test at least to have it as a practice test in order to get a true feeling of the examination. His tutor mentioned some of the popular grammar schools in that county, schools that my friend's Mum and mine had not considered before. Well, at least it meant more opportunities to get into a grammar school.

After five wonderful weeks in Mexico we had to come back to UK to get ready for the new school year.

Back to the UK it took us some days to go back to normal, we always suffer with jetlag and time difference but had to get used to quickly and continue with the 11+ preparation and this time it had to be every day.

September

School started in September and I for the first time was not happy with my new teacher in Year 6. So going to school was a big chore.

At school, I was given a diary for homework and 6 special books for the SATs preparation. I had to follow the diary and do pages of the books every day so they were marked at school the following morning. This was a bit of a shock to start with as I already had my 11+ work but after some time I just got used to.

Buckinghamshire Exam Details

Early September I got my first 11+ letter from the Buckinghamshire County Council. It acknowledge my registration to the exam and included the "GL Assessment Familiarisation and Practice Papers Verbal Reasoning Tests" for me to get some practice and familiarisation before the exam in October.
The letter had reference to the "guide to parents" and some websites to check for more information. It also indicated that they would contact us again with the details for the exam.

The 11+ exam for Buckinghamshire was going to consist of 2 verbal-reasoning multiple choice exams and the "familiarisation pack" included 3 verbal-reasoning test papers. I could not wait to start practicing with these papers so I opened the pack and did the first test. I did ok and got 66/80, I thought it was fine to be my first test paper.

The familiarisation pack was very useful as it had information about the 11+ test, tests, answer sheet, answers and explanation to the answers. I think they were very good level tests to start working with. They gave me confidence to keep working for the real test. Once again I got the new vocabulary and added it to my special list. Mum recorded my results on a progress chart she created for my tests.

After some days I started working with my Bond 11+ Test Papers Verbal and Non-Verbal Reasoning Multiple Choice and immediately noticed these were more difficult than the familiarisation pack from Buckinghamshire. I even needed extra time to complete my first Bond 11+ Test Paper.

From that day I started combining my Bond Assessment Papers and the GL Assessment 11+ Practice Papers. I also continued building up my vocabulary list.

My Mum also bought some other practice papers for me to try different type of questions and levels:

- IPS Eleven Plus Secondary School Selection Non-Verbal Reasoning Standard and Multiple Choice Dual Format.
- 11+ Verbal Reasoning Practice Test Papers Pack 2 Multiple Choice Version by Susan J. Daughtrey M. Ed.
- Secondary Selection Portfolio Test Pack Verbal Reasoning Multiple Choice Version by Athey Educational.
- Other tests from the internet.

This time I had to complete a test a day. My timings were not going very well but I decided to get used to the format of the tests and the new questions first.

I had some bad days when I did not want to do my 11+ work and preferred to rest but at that stage there was not time for that and my Mum was there to remind me of my duties.

When I was a bit tired or did not feel 100% I chose to work with any other test different from the Bond Test Papers as I personally found these more challenging and preferred to complete them when I was at my best.

St Bernard's Catholic Grammar School Exam Details

First week at school, I was given an invitation letter to the St Bernard's Catholic Grammar School introductory meeting for parents of prospective pupils on Thursday 16th September at 8:00 p.m. This meeting was going to be just for parents without pupils as pupils were going to be invited at a later stage.

The letter indicated that if my parents wished me to enter St Bernard's, they needed to complete a Common Application Form (CAF) supplied by my Local Authority (in my case Hillingdon) and a Registration Form, together with supplementary form A & B (commonly known as Priest Reference). It was drawing attention to the part of the Admission Policy that stated that priority would be given to baptised Roman Catholic children who had a written reference from their Roman Catholic priest and were successful in the 11+ examination.

The two test papers were going to be:

- A Non-Verbal Reasoning Paper, 50 minutes in length.
- A Verbal Reasoning Paper, 50 minutes in length.
- There was not going to be examination in Mathematics.

It indicated that GL Assessment (formerly known as NFER-NELSON) were standardising the papers to ensure that no children were unfairly helped or hindered because of their age.

Full length familiarisation test published by GL Assessment (complete with OMR sheets, answer sheets, parents' notes and marking instructions) could be purchased from WHSmith.

So my Mum completed the reply slip and booked her place for the introductory meeting.

St Bernard's Catholic Grammar School is part of a Consortium that includes Langley Grammar School and Herschel Grammar School therefore to apply for any or all of these schools you just need to complete one application form and sit just one set of exams. This is a shared examination process with these schools using the same examination papers for Non Verbal Reasoning and Verbal Reasoning tests.

Slough Grammar School has become part of the Consortium as well and you can now apply to this school with the Consortium application form and the Consortium exams.

So if you want to be considered for Langley Grammar, Herschel Grammar, Slough Grammar or St Bernard's Grammar you just need to sit one set of tests.

Settled down back into our routine, my Mum got on the internet to investigate all about the Buckinghamshire schools and tried to decide which ones were the closest to us as some of them were quite far from where I live.

Herschel Grammar Open Evening

During the first week of September I got a letter in my school from Herschel Grammar School.

The letter explained Herschel had transport with a pick up point close to where I live, lots of sports facilities and they were achieving wonderful academic results.

So we decided to attend their open evening. A friend and his mother came with us too.

I was excited to attend this open evening as it had been a long time since we visited Slough Grammar in April.

Around the 3rd week in September, we went to Herschel Grammar; we could notice it was very busy. We had to queue for a while before they opened the doors. Once inside we had to start our tour around the school because the hall was already full for the headteacher's speech.

Our tour was a long one but enjoyable, it is a lovely building with wonderful facilities, staff and pupils were very knowledgeable and approachable. It was a very nice experience.

You can really notice the difference between a grammar school and a non-selective school!

When we managed to get in the hall for the headteacher's speech it was still very busy. Thousands of people were visiting the school! The no bullying situation and the high A and GCSE's results got my attention.

Explanation about the 11+ exam was given. They also mentioned that 111 points were not enough to secure a place in Herschel Grammar and that all depended on the amount of children applying for places to this school and the points they could achieve.

They explained they are part of the consortium and just one set of application forms for the consortium were needed. They recommended to practice with the Verbal and Non-Verbal Multiple Choice GL Assessment 11+ Practice Papers. They were also selling them in one of the classrooms.

My Mum bought a couple of them to complete the sets with the ones I already had at home.

In the way back home my friend, his Mum, my Mum and I exchanged opinions and feelings about our visit. It was handy to have somebody else to talk about it, this way there were more people to pay attention to the visit and get more points of view.

Once again, we got the school prospectus and took notes of our visit.

Slough Grammar School Exam Details

Middle of September, I got a very nice and polite letter from Slough Grammar School confirming the receipt of my 11+ registration form. The letter was very clear and explained that for children in Slough Primary Schools the 11+ test was taking place on 6th November and for the other candidates, like me, the 11+ test was going to be held on 13th November. The letter explained what the test was going to consist of:

- A Non-Verbal multiple choice paper with 80 questions to answer in 40 minutes. This paper was going to consist of four sections each containing 20 questions to be answered in 10 minutes. Each section was going to have a worked example followed by two practice questions. Children were going to be told the correct answer to the practice questions and have a chance to ask any questions before beginning. Children were not going to get any warnings on this paper.
- The second part of the test was going to be a Verbal Reasoning multiple choice paper which was going to consist of 80 questions to answer in 50 minutes. This paper was not going to have practice questions but children were going to be given time warnings after 25 and 45 minutes.
- There was going to be a short break of about 20 minutes between the two papers.

They were going to write to us again in October to remind us about the test date, venue and registration point.

Now, because Slough Grammar School is part of the Consortium you do not need to do a separate exam like I did.

St Bernard's Catholic Grammar School Open Morning

On the 16th September my Mum and my friend's Mum attended the St Bernard's Catholic Grammar School introductory meeting that was mainly the Headteacher's speech. Mum commented it was quite interesting.

During the meeting parents were given the prospectus and application forms.

Explanation was given about the "consortium" and that we had to complete just one set of forms and hand it to the school of my first choice (of the consortium).

They also explained that passing the exam with 111 points did not warranty getting a place in St Bernard's and the example was a year before when only children with 113 points and above with the correct paper work and forms had been offered a place. The reason is that many children do the exam and pass with very good marks and because there are limited spaces in each school they get to select the children who passed with the most points.

A waiting list is available for the children who do not get offered a place and would like to wait in case a place comes available. In general, children can stay in the waiting list until December of their Year 7.

If you pass the exam, did not get offered a place and would like to enrol this school, request to be added to their waiting list as you may have a good chance to get a place or check if you can appeal as there have been cases when pupils get successful during this process and get offered a place in this school.

It is very convenient to check the admission criteria, the websites and prospectus for each one of the schools you think to apply for so you know exactly about the deadlines, time slots and forms to complete.

Mum had to send a reply slip to book a place to go to visit St Bernard's with me during one of their open mornings.

It was funny, most of my friends from school booked the same morning (Thursday 23rd September) to visit St Bernard's.

The day of our visit, we were taken to many classrooms by a group of students. I asked all my questions and found it was a very nice atmosphere to study. The building is a bit awkward as it is not a proposed building so you have to walk from one side to another in order to get to the different classes. The canteen is very small (most of the children end up bringing their own pack lunch and eating it in the playground or sitting on the hall floor) and the 6th form area is quite dated but staff and students are nice, very polite and you can see they are happy to be part of St Bernard's.

A few parents handed their application forms on the day of the open morning but receipts were not given. These were posted some days later.

We took back to school my friend and his mother and talked about our visit.

Langley Grammar Open Morning

More towards the end of September. At last, time to visit my last preferred school.

We opted to attend Langley Grammar School open morning rather than an open evening as you can get a better idea of the school by seeing the pupils in class, the school in action and during the day light. The open evenings are good but you do not get to see the real thing. I prefer to see the school in a normal day of classes than during a prepared opened evening without most of the pupils.

We listened to the headteacher, head boy and head girl's speeches in the hall and then were taken for a tour around the school.

Langley Grammar School has achieved higher A and GCSE levels than the rest of the consortium schools and has resulted on having much more demand from prospectus pupils. That makes it more difficult to get into Langley Grammar and a year before only children with 117 points or more were offered a place. This can explain the fierce competition and pressure around the 11+ exams.

As Langley Grammar School is part of the consortium, the exam was going to be the same as with St Bernard's and Herschel:

- A Non-Verbal Reasoning multiple choice Paper, 50 minutes in length.
- A Verbal Reasoning Paper multiple choice, 50 minutes in length.
- There was not going to be examination in Mathematics.

It was a lovely school, it had been refurbished recently, and the new sixth form building and dinning area were so spacious, smart and clean. The staff were very helpful and professional. Pupils looked enjoying being in the school. The atmosphere felt secure and happy.

I could see myself really loving being part of Langley Grammar. I knew from that day that Langley Grammar was going to be my first choice even though there was a big competition to get a place there.

My friend and his Mum came with us to Langley open morning and once again we talked about our visit all the way back to our primary school. They also liked Langley Grammar very much.

Burnham Grammar Open Evening

We visited Burnham Grammar School. People used to tell us that if we liked the consortium schools we were going to get very impressed by the Buckinghamshire grammar schools but it did not happen that way. The school was fine but we did not get that special feeling as when we visited the consortium and Slough schools. So I decided not to include it in my form. On the other hand, there were people who felt in loved with this school; of course it is always a very personal opinion and your own decision.

We did not visit any other Buckinghamshire grammar school as some open evenings dates clashed with my preferred schools open evenings and other times I was too tired from visiting other schools, doing my homework, 11+ preparations and my clubs.

The school visits can be very exhausting with all the walking around the schools, queuing, standing up for long periods of time and paying attention to all the details.

That is why it is much better to spread the school visits in two years or more rather than getting stressed and disappointed for not having enough days for all the visits.

Mum tried to book a visit to Dr Challoner's Grammar School but it was almost impossible to contact them. Eventually Mum got a reply and they responded they were not having any other visits to the schools apart from their open evening that we had missed. And because it is too far from my house I did not consider it.

My Mum sent my application form to take the 11+ exam at Langley Grammar for the consortium as I decided to have this as my first choice of the three schools. Mum also sent the faith forms signed and stamped by my parish's priest to St Bernard's to make sure I had all the papers in order in case I got offered a place in St Bernard's.

Common Application Form

During September, the "Common Application Form" (CAF) was available. This is the form that needs to be completed for the Local Authority where you live, in my case; I had to complete the Hillingdon CAF. That year the authorities insisted on forms to be completed on-line and just a few paper forms were available only by request.

My school sent a flier to each one of the children in Year 6. The flier had the important dates and the website address: www.eadmissions.org.uk

The important dates were: Friday 22nd October (closing date for applications to be submitted), 1st March (offer letters were going to be posted) and results were going to be ready on line on the same day from 5:00 p.m. and 15th March (deadline to send back the reply to the offer letter).

The Hillingdon CAF paper version looked like a book with detailed information on admissions for Hillingdon Borough and details of the secondary schools in the borough. It had a summary of the admissions criteria, important notes, additional information required, dates to supply the information for each school, statistical information, contact information and the "open evening dates". It is very useful information to assist you on the completion of the form and the decision making. An electronic version was available on the Hillingdon website.

The CAF is a form where you include your pupil information and indicate from 1 to 6 schools that you would prefer to go to in order of preference. You need to be very careful on the order you place your choices.

Make sure to check your Local Authority website for admissions information as sometimes they have different closing dates for specific situations.

If you are considering applying for a school that is not in your county you will have to contact the authority where the school you would like to apply is for information. The quickest and easiest way to do it is the internet.

My Mum got all the detailed information on each one of the school websites.

October

Another month! I was getting better. I could finish all my test papers in time and Mum did not need much time to mark them and get through the incorrect answers with me. This time I was able to explain what and why they were not right without having to see the explanation on the answers sheet.
In the first week of October we got a receipt from St Bernard's to confirm they had received my forms A + B.

On the 7th October I got my letter for Buckinghamshire 11+ test. As I live outside the county I was given 2 dates to sit the 2 different verbal-reasoning tests during the October half term (25th and 27th October) in Chesham Grammar School. I got the morning slots and had to register at 9:15 a.m. My Mum replied on-line confirming I was going to attend the test.

The letter also indicated that I did not need to bring any stationary with me, that I was going to be taken to the school hall and brought back approximately one hour later.

It indicated I needed to bring the letter to the test and had the option to bring my own watch into the testing session. No mobiles or drinks were allowed into the hall.

Going to the toilet before booking in was also advised as additional time was not allowed if children needed to visit the toilet during a test.

Parents were going to be asked to leave the building as soon as the child was booked in.

Details about parking and a map were included.

A paragraph indicated that there was going to be an opportunity for children who were ill to take the test at a later date.

Now it was getting closer and I had a date to focus on for my preparation.

One of my best friends also got the same dates and place to do his tests so I knew I was not going to be the only one from my primary school.

Early October, Slough Grammar School wrote to us with more details for the 11+ exam. My test was going to take place on Saturday 13th November and had to register between 8:45 a.m. and 9:00 a.m. I had to go to gate number 1. It indicated I was going to be collected from the gate by their Registration Point Advisors. My test was going to start as soon as possible after 9:00 a.m.

Once again, the letter was explaining the exam would consist of Non-Verbal Reasoning test with 80 questions in 40 minutes, a break of 20/25 minutes and a Verbal-Reasoning test with 80 questions in 50 minutes.

It indicated each room was going to have a clock and the invigilator was going to have a stopwatch. Rough paper would be given out to work out the answers.

I was asked to bring 2HB pencils, a rubber and a ruler, a drink and a snack to eat during the break.

My ID number was on the top right hand corner of the letter and I was requested to bring it to the test day.

The letter indicated that if I was ill on the day of the exam to inform them on the morning of the test or earlier in case of long-term illness so they could write to us with an alternative examination date.

Details about parking and a map were included as well.

Now I could picture myself going to the testing room and taking the test, it was kind of exciting and worrying at the same time.

On the week commencing 18th October, my Mum, Dad and I sat together to talk about what schools to include in my CAF as the deadline was getting very close.

It is a very important decision so you must think very carefully and make sure you talk lots about it, compare the schools, comment on your experiences with the visits to the schools and if possible get feedback from children and their parents who already go to those schools.

Finally, I had made my mind and we completed the form with the following preferred schools:

1. Langley Grammar
2. St Bernard's Grammar
3. Herschel Grammar
4. Slough Grammar
5. Bishopshall
6. Vyners

You must remember that the system will try to allocate the most top preference you indicate according to the different schools admission criteria and if you are not offered your first choice, your name is put on the waiting list for any of the schools that are higher preference than the one offered and the schools in lower preference than the one offered get removed. This is indicated in the offer letters like the one I got:

"Offers which could have been made for any schools which you placed lower in your preference list were automatically withdrawn under the co-ordinated admission arrangements, as a higher preference has been offered."

So if you pass the 11+ and place your grammar schools lower than a non-selective school or other and you qualify for those ones as well, then as the system will try to allocate the top preference and you may end up losing your chance to get in the grammar school.

Other case will be if you only chose grammar schools and then you fail the 11+, the system will then allocate you a secondary school that is not in your CAF but has a place available.

Please be very careful about your choices and the way you rank them. I have included my examples just as a guide but remember that admission criteria and admission process are constantly being updated.

Towards the end of the week, my Mum submitted my CAF on-line and got a password and a confirmation number.

By now, I was quite good answering my test papers in time and speeding up to leave some time to check the odd ones I did not know.

I was using my Mum's stop watch and working independently, I was managing my own test time and feeling more comfortable with the time I had for each test.

Now, I had to focus on passing the exams.

Note:

As a new Admissions Code became law on 1st February 2012, now schools have a duty to inform parents of the outcome of admission tests before the deadline for submission of the Common Application Form.

The Common Application Form must still be submitted by 31st October.

Some schools like the Consortium grammar schools will notify of the 11+ results the week commencing 22nd October 2012.

In order to have the 11+ results available for the new date, the 11+ test will be taken on 22nd September 2012 (sometimes before the Open Evenings

and Tours to the schools)

October half term

Talking to my Mum we decided I needed to go to a course to have a "warm up" with more children and feel the pressure of working with children of all levels in 11+.

My Mum got a flyer from a tuition company in Slough on the windscreen of the car on one of the grammar schools open evenings we attended. My Mum kept it and when she found out they were doing an intensive course during the half term, she phoned them and enrolled me.

One of my friend's Mums also decided to enrol my friend in the course even though he was already having private tuition during the week.

Therefore, instead of having a relaxing October half term I was working harder than on the normal school days but I was enjoying it and learning new things, and it was going to be just for a short time.

When I started my course I also saw two other children from my class who had joined to the intensive course.

That half term was very crucial and the amount of homework I was getting was tremendous. A few times I came back from the course, had dinner and sat down to complete my homework until 11:30 p.m. But I kept thinking that was going to be worthy and I was not doing that for a whole year, it was going to be just for a short period and it was one of the last chances I had to prepare for my exams.

During the intensive course, I got to work with more different test papers, asked some questions and learned some new techniques to answer them.

Because I was going to sit my Bucks exams I was going to miss two days of intensive course so I had to miss two days of football matches and go two Sundays to the intensive course to make up for the missed days.

Buckinghamshire 11+ Exam

I would advise you to take the Bucks exam or any other early exam as it is a good practice and it is another good opportunity to get in a grammar school. It gives you a real feeling of the exam and gives you an idea of what weaknesses you may have to correct them before your final 11+ exam.

A day before the Bucks 11+ test I started to get nervous, my Mum reminded me it was going to be just a practice and that I just needed to do my best.

On Monday 25th October I had to miss a day of intensive course but I was going to catch up on the Sundays. I woke up early, got ready and made sure my watch/chronometer and my stationary were ready.

A friend, his sister and his mother came with us as well. We all got to our designated school to take the exam: Chesham Grammar School.

We got there at about 8:30 a.m. It was very busy and after parking the car we all made our way to the school entrance. The doors were closed and had to wait outside. When they were ready at about 9:00 a.m., they opened the doors and we went inside to the registration desk where we had to show our exam letter. They asked us to wait around and they would call our names to go to the hall. Meanwhile we went to the toilet and found two other friends from our school who were going to do the exam with us.

After a while they called our names and we went into the hall. Our parents were asked to leave the school, they closed the school doors and we were ready to start the test.

I sat down at the desk that had my name on. We had to be very quiet, and then when the person indicated we could start there was not time to mess around. We had to go straight down to work. There were some questions I did not know and decided to spend some seconds reading them and then I left them out and did next questions and when there was little time left I went back to try to answer them and when there were just 50 seconds left I decided to take a guess. When the time was almost finished I told myself "it's ok I'll do well" and finished the exam.

When it is your turn to sit your exams, try to get rid of your worries while the test is given out, calm down and focus. Do your best. You will feel anxious and worried but try to be happy for having a chance to go to one of the best schools, remember that at the end everything will work out for you. Do not worry, it is hard to forecast what score or points you will get and do not pay attention to the others telling you it was a very easy exam for them. The time will tell when the results are given out.

When the test was over we were asked to hand it back and stand closer to the exit door and wait to see our adult (s) to leave the building.

When we were at the car pack I chatted to my friends comparing the answers we had.

Back at home, I spent a few hours finishing my intensive course homework.

On Wednesday 26th October I went to my intensive course and spent a few hours at home doing homework and went to bed early to get ready for the second Verbal Reasoning exam for Buckinghamshire.

On Thursday 27th October I got up early, got ready and checked my words list. My Mum got ready as well and we left to Chesham Grammar School with plenty of time.

This time I was feeling a bit more confident and relax as I knew what was going to happen. I was a bit familiar with the system. So again, we waited at the car park and when the doors of the school were opened I went to register myself at the desk and went to the toilet to make sure nothing was going to distract me during the exam.

I spotted my school friends and got together to talk about our expectations from this second exam. When our names were called we got into the hall and sat at the tables where our names were displayed.

Our parents were asked to leave and return in after an hour.

Some of the parents went back to their cars and waited there and others went to the next door sports centre for a coffee and waited in the centre's main entrance.

I set up my Mum's watch and got ready for the test. When the person indicated it was time to start I forgot about everybody and just concentrated on my test.

We were instructed not to talk or make any noise. We were so quiet that when one of the children dropped a pencil on the floor it sounded so loud that everybody could hear it.

The time warnings were given at 25 minutes and 45 minutes but with my watch on hand I could manage my time properly. I made the most of it and answered all the questions.

When the vigilator indicated to hand the tests back we had to finish and stood at the doors of the main entrance and left the building when we could see our parents.

When I joined my Mum I was happy that this stage was over and that this exam had given me a very good experience for the next exams. I felt positive about this exam and I regretted I had not included any of the Buckinghamshire grammar schools in my CAF.

I continued attending my intensive course for the rest of the half term and doing the extra homework.

On the last Sunday of the half term I went to my last intensive course day, we marked all the homework and had a big review. We were given a -good luck with your exams- card and said good bye to the instructors.

At the end of October I had finished all my GL Assessment 11+ Practice Papers and had re-done some of them. I worked on the other 11+ papers my Mum got me and the exams she found on the internet.

I enjoyed working with my Bond 11+ Test Papers, I found them difficult but I also noticed I learned very much with these. I considered the Bond Papers were closer to the real exams than the other papers I worked with.

November
Langley exam

Week commencing 1st November. The tension started to build up! That week I was going to sit my 11+ exam for the consortium and they were my first 3 preferred schools. This was going to be the real one! No more practice test. This was meaning my future. That week I decided to suspend all my after school activities and concentrate on doing more of my GL Assessment 11+ Practice Papers. I was doing two papers and my glossary every night. I also checked again some of my papers from the intensive course. My parents made sure I went to bed early.
On Thursday 4th November the children in Slough primary schools had been taking their 11+ Exam for the consortium in their own schools.

On Friday 5th November my Dad requested permission to school for me to stay at home and do the final revision. I woke up at usual time and spent some time doing more Bond 11+ Test Papers. I tried to relax and rest. At night, it was difficult to fall asleep, thoughts about my important test kept coming to my mind and my Mum had to give me a head massage. Mum talk to me very positively and told me once again it was not necessary for Mum and Dad I passed the exam that they were proud of me already, that they loved me and I just needed to do my best. Mum kept telling me that God would help us to get me into a good school. I eventually fell asleep.

On Saturday 6th November, I woke up early, got changed and ready for my test. All my family got ready as well. We had breakfast together and my Mum helped me to check I had my stationary, watch, snack, drink and exam letter ready. Mum lent me her watch/chronometer as I had been practicing with it during my preparation and I knew how to operate it. I also wore my first Holy Communion crucifix.

We all drove to Langley Grammar as that was my first choice of the consortium. We got there early and as we got to the car park there were school people telling us not to leave our car and wait in there as they were not ready yet.

One of my friends followed us to the school so we could get there together. He also had a blue examination registration form and had been assigned the same room number: 403.

We waited in our cars and saw so many cars coming immediately after us. People were not waiting in their cars and started making their way to the school building. It was incredible the amount of people that kept coming to the school.

After a while we decided to come out of the cars and followed everybody towards the school building. It was almost 9 o'clock and the exam was due to start in 30 minutes.

People concentrated in one building where they were getting drinks. We managed to find the toilets, then we looked for the registration room but there was not any.

My Dad decided to go back towards the car with my little brother as there too many people and he did not think it was convenient to have him there.

The few staff we managed to find told us to wait for people to call our colour paper. So we all went outside looking for staff among so many people, we guess there were around one thousand pupils plus parents. It was daunting! It was difficult to move around. So many children and so many colour examination registration forms they had! Eventually people started grouping so we looked for the person who was shouting and holding high a blue paper and when we got close enough to ask if we were in the right group she told us they were "light blue" forms and ours were "dark blue" forms! That was a shock! So many more types of colours and so many people!

People kept coming from everywhere and we continued walking around the building until we found the "dark blue" forms group, asked the person in charge and she confirm we were in the right group. It was then when we noticed that another of our friends from school was going to be sitting the exam. She had also had dark blue form but another room number.

Some groups of children started walking towards between the buildings and their parents were staying behind. Some staff were indicating that parents were not allowed passing that line and that they should go back to collect children in about 2 hours that children will be waiting in the same area.

Then it was time for my group to move. We all said bye to our parents got the final recommendations and blessings and went through.

My Mum went back to the car with my brother and Dad. They all went home. Some parents stayed in the waiting area or in their cars.

All the rooms were busy and places like library, hall and gymnasium were used to accommodate children for the exam.

When your turn to do your exams arrives, do not worry about others being smarter than you. Just remember everything you have learnt and try your best.

After the first test they gave us 10 minutes break that I used to recap and get positive. After the break they called us in. I just kept thinking positively and gave it my 100% and used my training from all my time studying and gave it all for every test.

When you go for your test, I would advise you to go to the toilet before the first test and during the break as there are not any other chances to do it. Remember to get to the test with plenty of time so you avoid getting stress with this.

Once they told us to stop the second test. We were instructed to hand the test and get our things ready to go back to our parents.

We were directed on how to leave the building and went back to the area where we left our parents. When we came out we were one of the last ones to finish so many parents and their children had gone already. There were just some parents waiting.

I got to see my Mum who gave me a big hug. I was relived; I had done one more of my main test!

We also got to know that my friend who had to sit her exam in another room had been very nervous, got very upset and had to be taken out of the room into another quieter room hoping this could help her to finish her exam. She could not cope with the pressure of the test: It was quite daunting and a big worry seeing so many children around.

The amount of children sitting the exams was frightening.

In the way home we commented about the big amount of children sitting the exam that day and Mum reminded us that one of her friend's daughters was going to sit her exam in the same school and same day but in the afternoon! So we could assume there were going to be the same amount of children later on. Imagine, over two thousand children sitting the exam for just 145 places! This really was a competition!

It had been a big experience being one of the two thousand children doing his best to gain a place for his preferred school.

At home, we all talked about the test and agreed it had been more difficult than the Buckinghamshire test. We just had to hope for the best.

My Mum spoke to other mothers whose children chose St Bernard's as their first choice and sat the exam there. They told Mum that there had been just something like 200 children sitting the exam and that no pressure was felt and the atmosphere there had been very calm and organised. That gave us a hope thinking there was not too much demand to get into St Bernard's and I could have a chance to get a place for my second choice.

Now I just had to keep preparing for my last examination.

Slough Grammar 11+ Exam

My Slough Grammar test was going to take place on Saturday 13th November and the week before I decided to study more and review the vocabulary and questions I remembered I was not very sure during the Langley test.
The children in Slough Primary Schools had already had their 11+ test in their own schools on 6th November.

I could definitively say that the GL Assessment 11+ Practice Papers were easy and were not at the same level as the 11+ exams. The Bond 11+ Test Papers were more difficult and at the same level as the real 11+ tests. So I decided to do more Bond 11+ Test Papers but my Mum could not get me any more multiple choice from the book shop as they were sold out and there was not much time to get them delivered home. So I practiced with the Bond 11+ Test Papers standard form. These can look a bit more challenging but they really helped me to raise my level.

I can tell you that they were the best papers I worked with as the Bond 11+ Test Papers really gave me a good level, close to the real exams. But I would recommend them after the GL Assessment 11+ Practice Papers to gain some confidence first and you do not get put off by the high level test papers at the beginning of your preparation.

I suspended all my after school activities that week to concentrate on my exam and made sure I was having plenty of rest.

Somehow I was a bit more relax this time, may be because I had already taken the 11+ examination for the consortium and those schools were my first choices.

On Saturday 13th November we all woke up early. I had my breakfast and checked my vocabulary list for the last time. My Mum asked me to check my stationary, watch, drink and snack that I was talking to the test.

My family and I left home with plenty of time in case of traffic around the school.

When we got there it was very busy and could not move to get to the car park so my Mum and I walked to the school gates where there were a couple of staff helping children to go through the gate as parents were not allowed to go through. A lady got closer to us and offered to help and when she saw my name written on the school letter she asked me where my surname came from I explained that my Mum was from Mexico then the lady introduced herself in Spanish. She was the headteacher of Slough Grammar! She was very nice and helpful. I waved bye to my Mum and went through.

When I got to the entrance I had to queue on the line for my surname initial and registered showing my examination letter then I was asked to wait.

I was sat down, waiting nervously and recapping on Verbal Reasoning when a member of staff called my number. I followed her into the classroom where she told me the sitting arrangement. After that she gave us the Verbal Reasoning test. I was very nervous but I tried my best up until the test was over.

We sat down and had our snacks, drinks and went to the toilet. I recapped on Non-Verbal Reasoning and calmed down.

Next, we had the Non-Verbal test. This time I had to come back to a few questions at the end to understand them. When the test finished I went to the playground to wait to be collected by my Dad.

My Dad went to pick me up. This time he drove through the back of the school and managed to leave the car in the car park. He walked with my little brother to the school gate where they had to wait for me as I was not ready.

In the way home I mentioned to my Dad it had been a good test and I felt I was going to get a good result for this one.

Now I was free! No more 11+ preparation and I could go back to my normal life and activities.

I was glad my tests were over and I just had to wait for my results on March 1st.

When I got back home, I felt strange no having to do more exams. The first week I had lots of spare time to do anything, on the second week I went back to my routine.

We could start talking about Christmas and look forward holidays.

Buckinghamshire results

We all knew the date for the Buckinghamshire 11+ results was getting closer. Parents and children could not stop talking about it.
On Thursday 25th November, I spent long time talking to Mum about how important it was for my future to get in a grammar school. I was not too worried about passing this exam because I had not included any grammar schools from Buckinghamshire in my CAF. I knew it had been a kind of "mock" exam but I was curious to know my results.

On Friday 26th November, I went to school as normal but I talked to my friends about the exams.

My Mum was nervous waiting to get the letter through the post with my results. As usual, the postman was late and my Mum did not get the letter while I was at school.

Some of my friends' mothers had contacted mine to ask about "the results" as they had received their letters and found out their children had not passed their exams.

Mum started to worry. All sort of worries crossed my Mum's mind.

Mum went to collect me at school and when we went back home, the first thing I noticed on the floor when I opened the door was "the letter". I did not even take time to close the door. I ran to the sofa and torn the envelope opened, pulled out the letter quickly and read through it just looking for my results. I got a final verbal reasoning test score of 119. And when I continued reading I understood I had not passed. I gave the letter to my Mum who read it properly and confirmed to me that I had not passed; that for Buckinghamshire the passing mark was 121! I got upset as I thought that was the easiest exam of the three I had done. I started thinking "if they were the easiest and I did not pass them, I could not expect passing the other exams".

After a while, we realised I had not lost much as I had not put any grammar schools from that county in my CAF.

Mum comforted me and tried to make me feel better and positive towards the other exams.

After the weekend, we went back to school. My friends and I exchanged our feelings of disappointments. We all thought we would have done much better.

December
Consortium results

It had been some time since we had our first results from Buckinghamshire. Now, the time was getting closer to the "second results" and my main results.
This time I was very worried, anxious and was not able to sleep for a few days. These results meant my future!

The night before 10th December, I stayed awake for a long time asking Mum: "what about if I do not pass the 11+ and I do not get a place in a good school in my borough as we do not live in the best catchment area?"

As always, Mum tried to make me feel confident, get me to relax and make me trust God would make things to happen in the best way. I finally fell asleep.

On Friday 10th October, I knew it was "the day". It did not matter what I did the whole day, I still kept thinking on the consequences my results would bring. I asked my Mum not to open my letter from Langley; I wanted to be the first one to read it.

I got to school and all my close friends could not stop talking about how anxious they were about getting the results.

My Mum was not working that day and went shopping trying to get distracted away from the 11+ results but when she was in the shops her mobile started ringing. My friends' mothers were calling my Mum to ask her about my results and told her all about their children's letters.

A girl who did the intensive course with me had passed with very good marks. One of my friends just managed to pass with 111 points and he was the one telling us it had been a very easy exam for him.

Mum went back home to check if the post had arrived but there was nothing.

The other mothers did not want to wait and opened their letters with the idea of preparing their children for the results in case of bad news.

Mum thought she could do the same but remembered I had asked her to let me open it first.

It was until about 3 p.m. when my letter was dropped through the letter box.

Mum saw the envelope and knew it was the results for my 11+ test. She wanted to open it but put it on the shelf and waited for me to come home.

Mum went to school to collect me.

When Mum was waiting for me at the playground, all the parents could not stop talking about the results.

A couple of my friends had failed and were very disappointed and my closest friends were excited with passing marks.

My Mum began to worry and thought: "what about if Tom has not passed?" I mentioned to her that the consortium's exams had been the most difficult ones.

That day I was having a friend coming to my house for a play for a couple of hours.

We got home and Mum showed me the envelope on the shelf but I did not want to open it while my friend was with us in case I had bad news, I did not want him to see me upset.

His Dad had phoned my Mum to tell her he had gone home early to open the envelope and read my friend had passed the exams. At that moment I wanted him to go home immediately to open my letter. I was not enjoying his company and I just wanted to be on my own.

The time passed so slowly. Eventually, my friend got picked up by his Dad who had brought the letter to show us the results. I did not want to tell them I was waiting for them to go to open my letter so I decided to tell them I was still waiting for the post. Finally, they left and quickly I got my letter from the shelf. My Mum offered to open it but I asked her to let me do it by myself then she offered to see me opening it but I said I did not want that so I walked to another room where nobody could see me. I tore the envelope opened and went directly to the paragraph of the results and found I had passed. I shouted: "I've passed, I've passed! I've got 117!" and ran to where my Mum was. Mum gave me a big hug and congratulated me. I told my Mum "now I know my future is bright!" She told me that was the reward to my hard work, dedication and effort. I was so delighted with my results. We were jumping with happiness.

I phoned Dad, my Grandparents in Mexico, my Grandparents in Coventry and all of them were so happy for me. They told me they knew I would pass.

That day I felt so relieved and with lots of confidence, my self-esteem was strong.

On the weekend, my Mum took me to see my favourite film: Harry Potter, on the special Cinemax screen. We enjoyed it very much.

On Monday back to school I could tell my friends about my results and I felt sorry for my friends who did not pass.

I could then look forward to spring so I could enjoy my treat for my very good 11+ results: a weekend in Alton Towers! But meanwhile I could enjoy the countdown to Christmas.

Slough result

On Wednesday 13th December, I had a normal day. I woke up, got ready for school and had an average day at school.

When we went back home and opened the door we found the letter from Slough Grammar. This was a bit of a surprise as we were not expecting this letter until the end of the week, but it was there in my hands.

I did not wait, I just opened the envelope and . . . good news! These were much better results: 124 points!

The very nice letter said "...we are delighted to tell you that your son has been deemed eligible for a place at this School for September...".

I was full of joy, now sure I was going to go to a grammar school. I had secured a place in one of my preferred grammar schools!

My Mum gave me a big hug and a kiss and could not stop telling me how proud and happy she was for me.

We talked about how worthy it had been all the hard work for the last 12 months, all the organisation and responsibility involved and the odd discussions my Mum had with me when she reminded me to study and I did not want to do it. Everything had been worthy and I was been paid off with my exam results.

Now sure I was going to be educated in a grammar school!

At school we all talked about our results and realised that I had done better than most of my friends who had tuition and private tutors. The success no just depends on the tutor but mainly on yourself, the atmosphere of the examination, and who supports you through it.

In my case I can say that my success was due to the following:

- God
- my own hard work
- my Mum
- the intensive course I attended in the October half term

Christmas and New Year

I have always loved Christmas holidays but this time it was special: I did not have to worry about 11+ preparation nor 11+ exams. I had my 11+ results and I knew I was going to a grammar school next year. I was so relaxed, happy and full of positive thoughts.

We had a week of snow during January. It was great to go out and play with the snow without any worry of having to do my 11+ homework. I was free to enjoy it to the maximum.

Back at school and settled into the new school term my class took part of the Primary Maths Challenge. We were paired to answer the test paper and after the teachers marked the papers my partner and I were informed that we had won the competition and were going to represent our school in the Borough's Maths Challenge. We were thrilled about it!

February

The new league tables were available on the internet and my preferred schools were mentioned on the top 200 secondary schools in the country! I was so glad I had chosen them.

I was so much looking forward to receiving the e-mail informing us of the school I would get offered.

I had been already looking up on the internet for my route plans to the four grammar schools I chose in my CAF: Langley, St Bernard's, Herschel and Slough. I found out where I could take the public transport and the time I would need to take the bus and how long it would take me. I just needed to know exactly what school I would be going to!

February half term. I decided not to enrol a holiday camp this time. Mum gave me information about some sports activities for half term but I decided to just relax and rest at home.

So, my brother and I spent time together playing on the consoles, the PC and in my kitchen. We enjoyed playing football and tag rugby in my kitchen. It is not very big but we managed to fit and had a good time playing with a soft ball.

The weather had not been great and we were forced to stay indoors. Mum took us swimming a couple of times, out for lunch, for walks in the shopping centre and played with us our favourite board games. A couple of times we went out to the park to the rides and played football but the rain made us go back home after some hours.

We enjoyed the break and did not want to go back to school but "the day" was getting closer: soon all the children in the UK were going to be informed of what secondary school place had been offered.

On Monday 28th February we went back to school. All my friends from class could not stop talking about the school they wished to get offered a place for. I had the feeling I will go to a grammar school but I wanted to know which one. I could not wait to start getting ready for secondary school!

At home I had been talking to Mum about wanting to know the news but she kept telling me we all had to wait to the following day. We continued talking about all the possibilities: if I got offered a place where my friends from school would not go, if some of my friends got offered a place in the same school as me, if I would mind not having my friends from school in the secondary school and so on.

March

Tuesday 1st March had arrived! But we had to wait until 5 p.m. to log on the admissions website and check the results. We had heard of previous years when many people tried to log on at the same time and the system had crashed. I hoped this time they had solved the problem and were prepared for all of us trying to find out about the schools at the same time. They had also informed that they would send the results by email but did not specify at what time. We knew that letters to all the applicants were going to be posted first class the same day so we should have had the letters from the following day.
Meanwhile I had to go to school and be patient. Mum would try to log on the system during the day to check if the results were sent before 5:00 p.m.

During the morning, an email was sent to my primary school informing the staff that the London Borough of Hillingdon had got it wrong and posted the result letters a day before and people were getting the letters the same day as the on-line results.

That morning, some of my Mum's friends started phoning her and texting her with their news. They were very glad but my Mum could not comment anything because she was at work and had not received the letter yet. Mum went home during her lunch break and found out the post had not arrived yet. Mum had to go back to work and my Dad went home to check.

In the afternoon, Dad contacted Mum to tell her the letter had arrived and asked her if she wanted him to open it. Mum could not wait and asked my Dad to open it and read it. When my Dad read I was offered my second choice: "St Bernard's Grammar School"; my Mum cried with joy. A big relief for all of us!

Mum wanted to find me at school and tell me the news but I had asked her to wait until I was back home so my Mum waited until we were at home and handed the letter to me. I started reading it slowly but I could not continue and just skipped to the part of "St Bernard's Grammar School" I was so delighted, I screamed: "yes, yes!"

My Mum then told me that there were other 4 friends from school who had been offered a place in the same secondary school. I got excited to imagine we can meet at some point in the new school. Now I could look forward to my new school and wait for the induction date and meeting at the school before starting in September.

I went to my mobile and sent texts to all my close friends telling them my news and asking them about theirs.

There was just one of my friends who got the highest 11+ score among us and did not get offered any of his choices. He got offered a school not mentioned on his CAF. He had chosen St Bernard's as his first choice. His Mum was devastated and very upset. They decided to wait to check on the admissions website in the evening. Sadly for my friend the website and email were the same as the letter. His Mum did not stop asking herself "why us?"

When my friend told us he did not get in St Bernard's we all knew there was something wrong and that sure he had to get a place in his first choice.

Meanwhile, another friend had a different situation. He got offered his second choice: Vyners. It supposed to be one of the best schools in the borough but his parents were not happy because they wanted their first choice: St Bernard's. So his father contacted the secondary school directly to ask why his son had not been offered a place and they told him that even though my friend had just managed to pass the test with 111 he did have a place in his first choice. His father explained that the letter from the borough was offering another school. Staff at St Bernard's told him that the Hillingdon borough was having problems and that some letters the borough had sent were incorrect. They advised him to wait for the letter the school was going to send home offering his son a place at St Bernard's and disregard the letter sent by the borough.

My friend's father told my other friend's Mum to phone the school because they might have received one of the incorrect letters the borough had sent.

My Mum's friends managed to contact St Bernard's after a long wait and engaged lines and they confirmed her son had a place at his first choice; again there had been an error in the borough's system.

We were all happy for my friends, now all of us who had passed the 11+ exam were going to the same school: St Bernard's Grammar school.

Now we just needed to wait for the offer letter coming directly from St Bernard's. At the end of the week we all got our offer letters, a reply form, a contact details form and a list of stationary we were going to need to start year 7 and the price to pay for stationary.

And with the same day's post there was a letter from Langley Grammar! We all wondered what it was. I quickly opened it and read it. It said I was in the waiting list as I had just missed the first round of offers for 1 point and that soon there was going to be a second round of offers. They were asking me to bear with them as they were just waiting to the first round replies and they were going to be offering more places. These were good news!

Since that day I was very excited, I would rather going to Langley Grammar than St Bernard's.

Mum went on researching about the two schools trying to find out all the pros and cons of each one while waiting for Langley to inform us if I got a place in the second round. Mum asked Langley if she should accept the place that I had been offered at St Bernard's and the staff at Langley advised her to accept the place to make sure I got into a school while I was waiting. So my Mum replied to St Bernard's and accepted the place.

Days had gone. I had been chatting to my friends at school who were very happy to go to St Bernard's. But I am good at Maths, love ICT and sports and Langley Grammar is a better school and has Maths and computing specialisation apart from many other awards. So I thought Langley would be best for me. I was not going to go to St Bernard's just because my friends were going to go there, this time I had to think about my future and knew I am quite capable of making new friends so I told my Mum and agreed that if I did not get offered a place in Langley my parents would appeal to try to get me into my 1st choice school.

Meanwhile, I had to keep preparing for the SATs and another violin exam.

On Tuesday 16th March Mum received a call from Langley Grammar school to ask her if we were still interested on a place in their school. Mum immediately told the lady on the phone we were and then the lady said she was sending a confirmed offer of a place in Langley Grammar through the post and that it would arrive in two days time.

My Mum told me about the news after school. I was over the moon, first I could not believe it but then I realised it was true. My Mum gave me a big hug and lots of kisses. She started calling me "Niño Langley" that means Langley boy.

I immediately got my mobile and texted my friends with the big news. It had been a surprise to all of them as everybody knew that it was a big thing to get into a top grammar school. Langley Grammar was in position 22 of the top 200 secondary schools in the country, according to the BBC Secondary league tables: Best GCSE results on 12 January 2011.

A couple of days later we received the offer letter from Langley Grammar. Mum sent the reply the next day and phoned the school to confirm they had received it.

Since then I could not stop thinking and talking about how it would be to wear Langley uniform, be in the school, study my favourite subjects: Maths and ICT and the rest of the subjects.

Another of my friends who got 116 points was in the waiting list for Langley and so far in position 6. We thought he would get an offer in 2-3 weeks time but he had his doubts as he thought he would struggle to work hard and keep up with the level in Langley and not in St Bernard's. Well, it was up to him to make up his mind. I was sure I wanted to learn, make new friends and make the most of this opportunity.

Now I could look forward to my bright future.

On 24th March I represented my school in the London Borough of Hillingdon Primary Maths Challenge. It took place at the Council Chambers Civic Centre Uxbridge. It was quite an honour to be there among so many clever children. We were explained that we were 104 children selected out of 5,500 children in the entire Borough. It was a great experience.

April - July

We worked hard towards the SATs in May, were given lots of homework and at a lot of mock tests.
All you could hear my teacher talking about was "SATs".

In May, I sat my SATs exams that were easier that any of my 11+ exams. Doing my 11+ exams was a fantastic experience and helped me mature and learn to cope with pressure. When I sat my SATs I was relaxed and knew how to focus even thought I was cover with chicken pox for the whole week of SATs. I also knew that these were not as important as the 11+ and my future did not depend on these. My future was already sorted.

Once the SATs were over school was just a recap, fun activities and preparation for our big trip.

In June we had our wonderful trip to Wind Mill. We all loved it and had lots of outdoors activities and some late nights. Three days trip were not enough and we would have preferred to stay for a whole week.

Back to school we started to have our induction meetings for parents and induction days for pupils in our secondary schools.

My friend who was in the waiting list for Langley got offered a place at the beginning of July but decided to go with the flow and stayed in St Bernard's.

. . .

Hope these pages have given you an idea of what the process of the 11+ exam is and guide you through how I prepared to achieve the score needed to get into my preferred grammar school.

I am so happy I took the opportunity to sit the 11+ exams.

I am so relieved, happy and proud it is all over and I have achieved what I worked so hard for.

My Mum will have a break for a while and when my little brother turns 6 years she will start couching him with the Bond Assessment Papers. In this way, my brother will get familiarised with the "Verbal" and "Non-Verbal" reasoning concepts with a more paced schedule, and when he gets to Year 5 it should be easier for him to prepare for his 11+ exams. We hope we can get him into Langley Grammar as well!

I hope that when it is your turn to go through the 11+ process you also get a positive and great experience of it.

My best wishes and hope you also get a bright future.

Glossary

<u>11+</u>

According to Wikipedia: "In the United Kingdom, the **11-plus** or **Eleven plus** is an examination administered to some students in their last year of primary education, governing admission to various types of secondary school. The name derives from the age group for secondary entry: 11–12 years. The *Eleven Plus* examination was once used throughout the UK but is now only used in a number of counties and boroughs in England. The *Transfer Test* examination tests a student's ability to solve problems using verbal reasoning, mathematics and non-verbal reasoning and English."

According to Bond, The Parents' Mini Guide to the 11+: "The 11+ is a selective entrance exam that determines which children will be offered a place at a UK grammar school.

Taken in Year 6, the tests are not compulsory and do not have a specific pass mark.

Under some Local Education Authorities (LEAs) the 11+ is available for all Year 6 children and is taken in class. In others it is organized by the school or on a weekend at the secondary school.

The exam differs across the country in terms of the subjects taken and the examining board used. The test can be multiple choice or standard format and can contain up to four subject areas."

Verbal reasoning

From Wikipedia: "Verbal reasoning is understanding and reasoning using concepts framed in words. It aims at evaluating ability to think constructively, rather than at simple fluency or vocabulary recognition."

According to Bond, The Parents' Mini Guide to the 11: "Verbal Reasoning is seen as a reliable indicator of potential academic ability. It tests a child's aptitude for problem solving as well as their capacity to process verbal information effectively.

A test paper can include a wide range of question types within the following core areas:

- Sorting words
- Selecting words
- Anagrams
- Coded sequences"

Non-verbal reasoning

According to Bond, The Parents' Mini Guide to the 11: "Non-verbal Reasoning is perceived by many schools as an effective gauge of natural ability. It relies largely on logic and the analysis of graphic information rather than literacy skills or an understanding of verbal processes.

A test paper can include a wide range of questions within the following core areas:

- Identifying shapes
- Rotating shapes
- Missing shapes
- Coded shapes"

Multiple choice paper

From Bond, How to do...11+ Verbal Reasoning: "Children will need to choose their answer from a set of options and mark it on a separate answer sheet. It is often easier to work out answers using this format as the answer must be one of the given options for each question. However, children must mark their answers very carefully as the answer sheets are often read and marked by a computerised system."

Standard format paper

From Bond, How to do...11+ Verbal Reasoning: "In the standard format, answer options are not given. Children must find each answer and write it directly onto the question paper."

Standardisation

According to elevenplusexams.co.uk. : "One of the most common causes of confusion about the 11 Plus are the terms 'standardised score' and 'age standardisation'. Parents struggle to understand how, when a paper may have 80 questions on it, the final score they are given can be a figure of, say, 130.

What follows here is a very simplified explanation of the process of standardising scores.

Standardisation is a statistical process that is designed to take account of two factors:

- Firstly, the number of questions on a test paper and the time allowed for it can differ. If a Verbal Reasoning test has 80 questions and takes 50 minutes, while a maths paper has 100 questions and takes 45 minutes, simply adding the 'raw scores' of the two together will not give equal weight to the results of both tests, and nor will an average. Standardisation is a way of giving equal value to the results of each test, regardless of the number of questions and the time allotted for completing them.

- Secondly, and possibly of more concern to parents, the test scores have to be adjusted to take account of their age at the time they take the 11+. One child taking the test might be born on the first day of the school year (September 1st) while another might be born on the last day (August 31st). With what amounts to a whole year's difference in their ages, the older child is clearly at an advantage: as just one example they will have a whole additional year's vocabulary, which the younger child will not. As children are exposed to new vocabulary at the rate of more than 1,000 words per year, the difference can be very significant for the 11+ tests. In order to remove this unfairness, the marks are adjusted to make them "standard" for all children, regardless of their age.

If both children in this example – the oldest one and the youngest one – achieve the identical 'raw score', the youngest child's final 11+ score will be higher than that of the oldest child. The standardisation process has 'awarded' extra marks to the younger child to compensate for their younger age. Every test paper is unique in the factors that go into standardising it but if both children achieved a raw score of 75/80, a very rough outcome could be that the older child's standardised score might be approximately 133, while the younger child's score could be around 136. (Please note that these figures are given as examples only and do not represent actual marks.)"